TOTAL SURRENDER

GIVING EVERYTHING TO GOD

THIS BOOK BELONGS TO: Natasha ♡

DATE STARTED: ~~6/23/24~~ 6/24/24

PUBLISHED BY YM360

TOTAL SURRENDER: GIVING EVERYTHING TO GOD
©2024 by youthministry360. All rights reserved.

Published by YM360 in the United States of America.

ISBN 13: 9781954429451

No part of this publication may be reproduced, stored in a retrieval system, or transmitted in any form or by any means electronic or mechanical, including photocopy, recording, or any information storage and retrieval system now known or to be invented, without prior permission in writing from the publisher.

Any reference within this piece to Internet addresses of websites not under the administration of YM360 is not to be taken as an endorsement of these websites by YM360; neither does YM360 vouch for their content.

Unless otherwise noted, scripture quotations are from the ESV® Bible (The Holy Bible, English Standard Version®), © 2001 by Crossway, a publishing ministry of Good News Publishers. Used by permission. All rights reserved.

The Holy Bible, New Living Translation, © 1996, 2004, 2015 by Tyndale House Foundation. Used by permission of Tyndale House Publishers, Inc. All rights reserved.

Author: Amber Warren
Design: FTN Design, Morgan Williams

TABLE OF CONTENTS

Total Surrender Intro	4
Large Group Session 1 Notes	6
Small Group Session 1 Intro	8
Session 1 Getting Started	9
Session 1 Digging In	10
Session 1 Wrapping Up	12
Large Group Session 2 Notes	14
Small Group Session 2 Intro	16
Session 2 Getting Started	17
Session 2 Digging In	18
Session 2 Wrapping Up	20
Large Group Session 3 Notes	22
Small Group Session 3 Intro	24
Session 3 Getting Started	25
Session 3 Digging In	26
Session 3 Wrapping Up	28
Large Group Session 4 Notes	30
Small Group Session 4 Intro	32
Session 4 Getting Started	33
Session 4 Digging In	34
Session 4 Wrapping Up	36
Totoal Surrender Closing	37
Devotion 1	38
Devotion 2	40
Devotion 3	42
Devotion 4	44
How To Know Jesus	46
Acknowledgements	47

INTRODUCTION

Total Surrender. Sounds a little scary, doesn't it?

Throughout history, we read of people and nations that have surrendered in battle. We have seen movies where heroes and villains alike surrender their lives, their power, and their causes. And despite all of these examples of surrender as loss, we have read stories and heard songs about sweet surrender. The kind of surrender that feels effortless. And that may cause you to wonder, which one describes our relationship with God?

As you flip through this book and spend time talking about Total Surrender, what you will come to find is that God is asking for every single portion of our lives. He wants our full attention, every day and all day. And unlike the surrender we see at the end of a battle, God doesn't benefit from our surrender. Think about it- God doesn't really need anything we have to build His own wealth. He desires our total surrender, because He has far more to give us than we have to give Him.

When we surrender our life to Christ, it is not the end. It is the beginning of a new life- one that lasts forever.

GALATIANS 2:20

I HAVE BEEN CRUCIFIED WITH CHRIST. IT IS NO LONGER I WHO LIVE, BUT CHRIST WHO LIVES IN ME. AND THE LIFE I NOW LIVE IN THE FLESH I LIVE BY FAITH IN THE SON OF GOD, WHO LOVED ME AND GAVE HIMSELF FOR ME.

LARGE GROUP

These two pages are designed for you to take notes during Large Group Sessions. The stuff you're learning will build on itself over the next few sessions. So even if you're not much of a note-taker, you might want to at least jot down what you think is important.

TRY WRITING DOWN THE FOLLOWING
- Any specific teaching points
- Verse references for Scripture passages
- Quotes that make you think
- Anything you have a question about

NOTES
SESSION 1

SMALL GROUP SESSION 1
INTRODUCTION

When you go about your day, do you ever consider what drives the decisions you make?

Maybe there are desires in your life that drive certain decisions. For example, you may want to become a professional musician and to do so, you may decide to practice your instrument for an hour or two each day.

Or it could be people in your life that influence your decisions. Some people are very influenced by their friends, and will make decisions like what classes to take based on who all they can take them with.

So imagine for a moment how crazy it would be to totally surrender all of these decisions to God. Imagine that from the time you woke up until the time you fall asleep, you were making decisions solely based on God's desire for your life, rather than your own understanding or the influence of your friends and family.

It has the potential to change everything. And that is just what God wants for you!

GETTING STARTED — SESSION 1

In this exercise, you are going to be looking at a few different areas of your life. With your group, work through each area and fill in your answers below.

Your Money ____Parents____

What Clothes Are In Your Closet ____Me____

Your Lunch ____Me____

The Time You Wake Up ____Me & my dogs____

Which After-School Activities You Do ____Me & my parents____

Where You Live ____Parents____

The Decorations In Your Room ____Me____

Your Phone Background ____Me____

SESSION 1
DIGGING IN

Work together with your group to dig in to these passages.

TOTAL SURRENDER AND THE RICH YOUNG RULER

READ MARK 10:17-18 WITH YOUR GROUP.

What are some things that we often mistake for God? In other words, what are some things that we are tempted to give ultimate authority to instead of God?

> ~~[scribbled out]~~ Intimate relationship
>
> You can recognize Jesus without knowing him.

Why is it important to understand who Jesus is?

> Jesus is God!

READ MARK 10:21-22 WITH YOUR GROUP.

What surprises you about the Jesus' response? What does it make you feel about Him?

> Jesus is compassionate & loving, knew what was controlling him, is loving

What surprises you about the rich young ruler's response? What does it make you feel about him?

Take a few minutes to reflect.

- What are some things that you would struggle to give away?

  Phone/electronics, ~~m~~ relationships, ego

- How would it look for you to totally surrender everything in your life to Jesus?

  Becoming complete humble & more wise with God's wisdom

NOW, READ MATTHEW 22:34-40 WITH YOUR GROUP.

Consider what Jesus is asking for in this passage, and write down some of the ways you can totally surrender in each of these categories below.

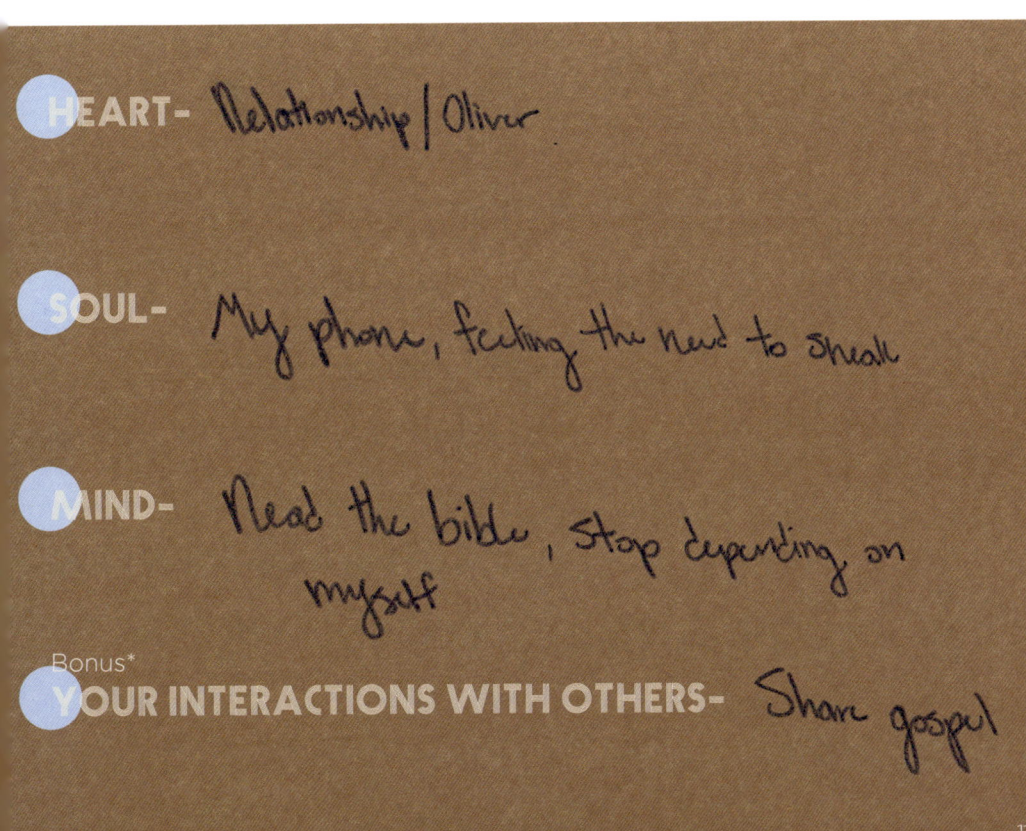

HEART- *Relationship/Oliver*

SOUL- *My phone, feeling the need to sneak*

MIND- *Read the bible, stop depending on myself*

Bonus*
YOUR INTERACTIONS WITH OTHERS- *Share gospel*

WRAPPING UP

SESSION 1

Instructions: With your group, fill in the graph below with some specific things that you want to totally surrender to God. And to the right of each thing, write down what that might look like in your life long-term.

I want to totally surrender _____ to God	That looks like_____
Staying up	Studying my bible instead
Initimate relationships	Finding someone that loves God & loves me like God wants
Being embarrassed about Christian / God	Talking about God & building a relationship with Hi-
Worldy desires/pleasures	Becoming more stern & filled with God's wisdom

MARK 10:29-30

Jesus said, "Truly, I say to you, there is no one who has left house or brothers or sisters or mother or father or children or lands, for my sake and for the gospel, who will not receive a hundredfold now in this time, houses and brothers and sisters and mothers and children and lands, with persecutions, and in the age to come eternal life."

LARGE GROUP NOTES — SESSION 2

These two pages are designed for you to take notes during Large Group Sessions. The stuff you're learning will build on itself over the next few sessions. So even if you're not much of a note-taker, you might want to at least jot down what you think is important.

TRY WRITING DOWN THE FOLLOWING
- Any specific teaching points
- Verse references for Scripture passages
- Quotes that make you think
- Anything you have a question about

★ Romans 10:9-10 for reassurance

★ Galatians 2:16

Justified = Jesus treats me like "I've never sinned"

1. Faith makes us righteous
   - Trust / belief
   - In the work of God
   - know the difference between demons & Satan

Faith in Jesus Christ makes us righteous

Noah arks — Waters = God's judgement
Arks = Those in Christ

SMALL GROUP INTRO
SESSION 2

Have you ever felt like there are some things that you will never be able to do? For example, you may be the kind of person who would be more than happy to go sky-diving. But odds are, you are more likely to be one of the many people who are confident that they will NOT be jumping out of a plane with only a back pack to save them.

In this session, we are going to talk about something that you absolutely can not do- be righteous. Righteousness is a word we hear often in Christian circles, and it can be tricky to understand. That's why our goal for this session is to understand what righteousness is and why we can only have it by totally surrendering to God.

GETTING STARTED — SESSION 2

Great news! You can have each of these three things! The only catch? You have to pick three of the four things listed below to go along with it. Choose wisely.

1. SOMEONE IS GIVING YOU A BRAND-NEW VEHICLE OF YOUR CHOICE, WITH AN UNLIMITED BUDGET FOR ACCESSORIES AND CUSTOMIZATIONS!

You cannot drive it to any concerts or games for the next five years	✓ You have to use it to drive an elderly person to church every Sunday morning
✓ You have to do all of the repairs on it yourself (Not pay for them...actually repair them yourself)	✓ You have to use it to go on a 3-day road trip with the most annoying person you know.

2. IT FINALLY HAPPENED— YOU ARE A SOCIAL MEDIA INFLUENCER WITH 1.2 MILLION FOLLOWERS.

✓ You must spend 35 hours each week working on the content that you post (along with your other responsibilities)	✓ You are legally required to use the phrase "whatever floats your boat" at least twice on every post
You must miss a lot of school, and to keep up, you hire a tutor that smells strongly of sour milk.	✓ Each month, a group of trolls post several videos talking poorly about you.

3. NEXT SUMMER, YOU ARE GOING TO SPEND TWO MONTHS AT THE DESTINATION OF YOUR DREAMS. ROOM, BOARD, AND FUN ACTIVITIES ARE ALL INCLUDED.

✓ You can't take your cell phone or laptop with you.	✓ You can never return to this place after you leave at the end of the summer.
You can only take one outfit to wear the entire summer.	✓ You have to read 25 books about the place that you are visiting before you leave.

DIGGING IN
SESSION 2

RIGHTEOUS	UNRIGHTEOUS
Being honest	Suppressing/hiding the truth
Fully surrendering	~~scratched out~~
Honoring God	Intentional acts
Compassionate	Making idols
Being humble in ourselves	Acting foolishly
~~Worship~~	Not honoring God
Worshipping God	Not being thankful
Humble, open mind & heart	Acting wise
Respectful & honest	~~Ha~~ Having a ~~dark~~ darkened heart
Positive & grateful	Making their own Gods
	Being filled with Covetousness, Maliciousness, haters of God, full of envy, deceit, backbiters, despiteful, boasters

Fill in the blanks with your group and answer the questions below.

1. ___None___ is righteous, no, not one. (Romans 3:10)

    - When you look at your 'Unrighteous' column on the previous page, do you see areas where you have thought or acted unrighteously? What about other people? Can you think of ways that they have been unrighteous?

    - Imagine living a completely righteous life. Do you think that would be difficult? Why or why not?

2. For our sake, He made Him [Jesus] to be ___sin___ who knew no ___sin___, so that in Him we might become the ___righteousness___ of God. (2 Corinthians 5:21)

    - How does it make you feel to know that even though you can not obtain righteousness on your own, God made a way for you to become righteous by faith in Jesus Christ?

    - When you come to faith and 'become the righteousness of God,' how should your actions change?

3. I appeal to you therefore, brothers, by the mercies of God, to _____ your bodies as a living sacrifice, holy and acceptable to God, which is your _____ _____. (Romans 12:1)

    - Read Romans 12:2 with your group and write down your thoughts here.

    - Have you ever done something that most people would say is good, but you had bad motives for doing it? What was it, and how did it make you feel afterward?

WRAPPING UP SESSION 2

Read Matthew 23:27-28 with your group.

Once done, look at the image below. There is room in the 'white-washed tomb' for you to write down some things that you try to present to the world. Then, below the tomb, write down some things that you've buried away and don't want others to see.

Once you are done writing some things down, spend time thinking about what it would look like to surrender all of that to Jesus.

2 CORINTHIANS 5:21

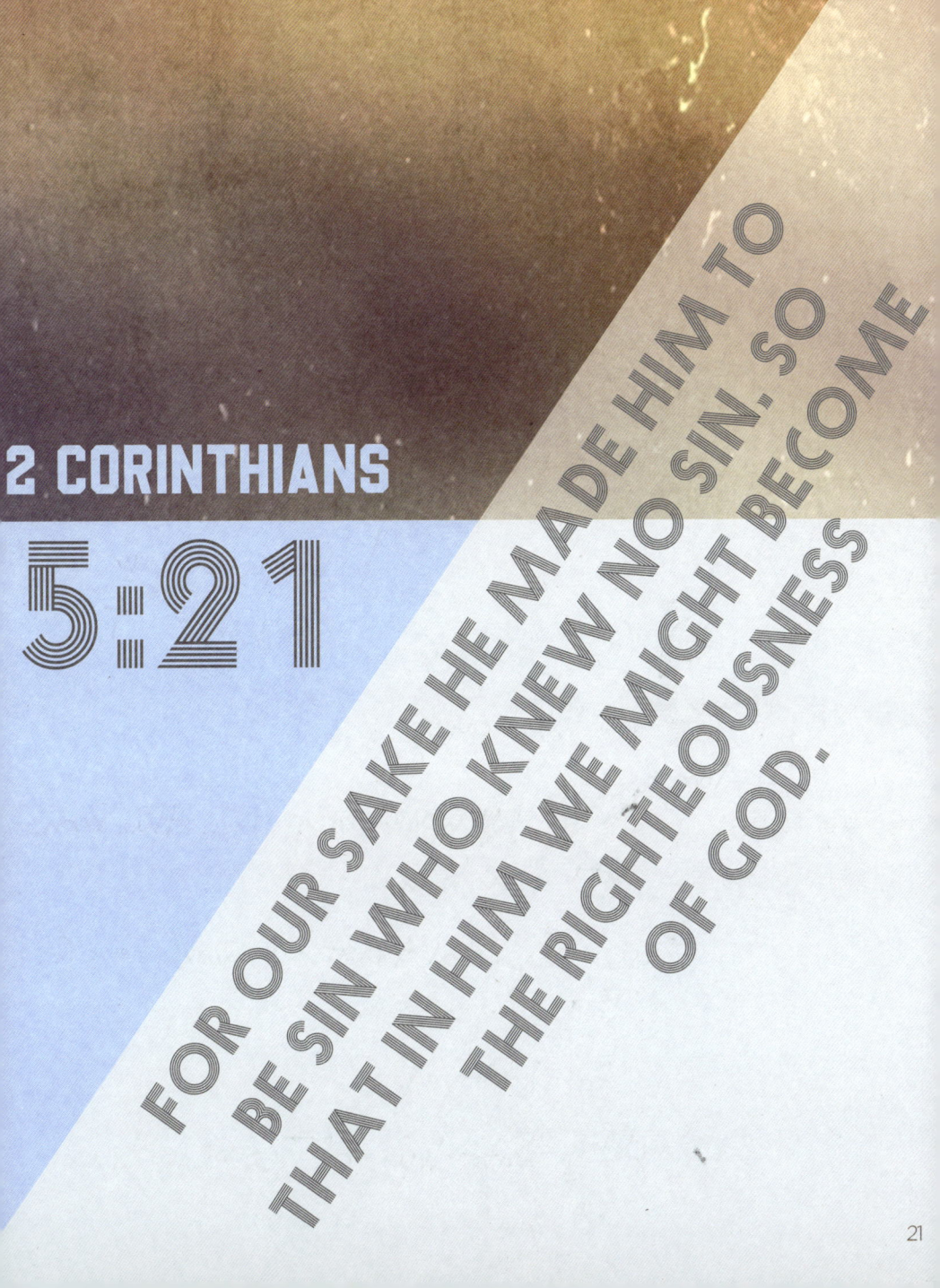

For our sake he made him to be sin who knew no sin, so that in him we might become the righteousness of God.

LARGE GROUP

These two pages are designed for you to take notes during Large Group Sessions. The stuff you're learning will build on itself over the next few sessions. So even if you're not much of a note-taker, you might want to at least jot down what you think is important.

TRY WRITING DOWN THE FOLLOWING
- Any specific teaching points
- Verse references for Scripture passages
- Quotes that make you think
- Anything you have a question about

※ Mark 12: 28-34

What will you give your life to?

Cruciform life - life that love God & love your neighbor — †

1.) Grow to love God holistically

longer ~~~~ you walk with God, the more you love him

Soul - Spiritual trust & reliance on God

To know your sin doesn't stop God from loving you.

Anything that's true of Jesus, is true of you

NOTES
SESSION 3

Mind - Diligent study to know h [scribble] love God

love God with your mind

Strength - Using your body to make God known

2.) loving your neighbor as yourself, then you love God

Give your live to God holistically h loving thu needy

SMALL GROUP SESSION 3 INTRODUCTION

At some point in your walk with God you will ask yourself if following God's ways are really the best thing for your life. After all, you may have friends and family members that are living in ways that do not honor God... and yet they seem really happy. It can be difficult to do something with no reason other than doing it because 'Jesus said so.' These are the moments where total surrender starts to really feel like giving up everything.

In this session, we are going to talk about the daily commitment we make to following Christ. There is no secret in your mind and heart that your behavior will not display in some way. That is why when we talk about living a life surrendered to God, we are talking about more than 'doing the right thing' or 'saying the right words.' We are talking about changing our hearts and minds to fully reflect our relationship with God!

GETTING STARTED — SESSION 3

With your group, think back to when you learned to do each of these things, and the specific way that you were taught to do them. Fill in the blanks and answer the questions below!

1. _____*Dad*_____ taught me to play tic-tac-toe.

    a. Where on the tic-tac-toe board did they tell you was the best place to put your first move?
    Edges

    b. Who did they tell you goes first, X or O? Or does it matter?
    Doesn't matter

2. _____*Parents*_____ showed me how to make a bowl of cereal.

    a. Which is correct: Milk first, Cereal first, or No Milk?
    Cereal first

    b. Is cereal a breakfast-only food or an anytime snack/meal?
    Anytime snack/meal

3. _____*Parents*_____ taught me how to start a difficult conversation.

    a. When you approach someone that has upset you, is it better or worse to try and make them laugh first?
    Worse

    b. In most cases, is it better to address an issue as soon as it arises, or to give yourself some time before you bring it up?
    Give myself time

SESSION 3
DIGGING IN

Work together with your group to dig in to these passages.

And he said to all, "If anyone would come after me, let him deny himself and take up his cross daily and follow me. For whoever would save his life will lose it, but whoever loses his life for my sake will save it. For what does it profit a man if he gains the whole world and loses or forfeits himself?"
- Luke 9:23-25

Who is God asking to deny themselves?

> Sinners/ourselves

But I say, walk by the Spirit, and you will not gratify the desires of the flesh. For the desires of the flesh are against the Spirit, and the desires of the Spirit are against the flesh, for these are opposed to each other, to keep you from doing the things you want to do. But if you are led by the Spirit, you are not under the law. – Galatians 5:16-18

Who keeps us from gratifying the desires of our flesh?

> Holy Spirit

Now the works of the flesh are evident: sexual immorality, impurity, sensuality, idolatry, sorcery, enmity, strife, jealousy, fits of anger, rivalries, dissensions, divisions, envy, drunkenness, orgies, and things like these. I warn you, as I warned you before, that those who do such things will not inherit the kingdom of God. – Galatians 5:19-21

Keep in mind here, that Paul is talking to a group of people who have already claimed to totally surrender to Jesus. And yet, they are still meeting their needs with their fleshly desires. Why do you think it was a big deal to Paul that they stop doing these things?

> Against God's will

It is very tempting to meet our needs with sin rather than God. Take a moment to look at the list, and think about what needs these sins might be meeting. For example: if your need is to feel safe, you may seek that safety by trying to control others (sinful/fleshly desire). And giving into that fleshly desire might look like throwing a fit of anger so they are so scared they do what you want. What are some other needs that we improperly meet with sin?

lovebombing / lying

> But the fruit of the Spirit is love, joy, peace, patience, kindness, goodness, faithfulness, gentleness, self-control; against such things there is no law. And those who belong to Christ Jesus have crucified the flesh with its passions and desires. If we live by the Spirit, let us also keep in step with the Spirit. Let us not become conceited, provoking one another, envying one another.
> – Galatians 5:22-26

Have you totally surrendered to God in your mind, body, and soul? Or are you still hanging on to the sins that your flesh desires?

haven't totally surrendered yet

> Therefore, preparing your minds for action, and being sober-minded, set your hope fully on the grace that will be brought to you at the revelation of Jesus Christ. As obedient children, do not be conformed to the passions of your former ignorance, but as he who called you is holy, you also be holy in all your conduct. – 1 Peter 4:13-15

What are some areas of your life that do not feel fully surrendered to God? What steps could you take today that will help you set your hope fully on God?

Intimate relationships

WRAPPING UP

SESSION 3

	The World Says...	**God Says...**
James 1:5	Wisdom is only found when we 'truly know ourselves' and it can be different for different people.	Wisdom is found in _God_
James 1:14	Temptation is a way that we are tested. It comes when the Devil wants to trip us up or when somebody else does something to entice us.	Temptation comes from _man_
James 4:1	Your desires are who you truly are inside. You should always fulfil them if you want true happiness. You can't control what you want. You know what's best for you.	Our passions are _desires_ within us. (Read James 4:2-3 to understand what this leads to)

One of the best ways to start totally surrendering your mind, body, and soul to the Lord is to understand the key differences between what the world tells you to do with yourself and what God calls you to do.

JAMES 4:7-8

SUBMIT YOURSELVES THEREFORE TO GOD. RESIST THE DEVIL, AND HE WILL FLEE FROM YOU. DRAW NEAR TO GOD, AND HE WILL DRAW NEAR TO YOU. CLEANSE YOUR HANDS, YOU SINNERS, AND PURIFY YOUR HEARTS, YOU DOUBLE-MINDED.

LARGE GROUP NOTES
SESSION 4

These two pages are designed for you to take notes during Large Group Sessions. This is your final Large Group Session. Even if you are not much of a note-taker, you may want to jot down your final thoughts on this study.

TRY WRITING DOWN THE FOLLOWING
- Any specific teaching points
- Verse references for Scripture passages
- Quotes that make you think
- Anything you have a question about

✱ Jeremiah 29:11-14

✱ The greatest & most fruitful ministries will be the product of the deepest wounds

1.) Failure <u>doesn't</u> have the final word

God will use failures & successes ~~to be~~ to bless his people

"Seek me with your whole being"

2.) God uses it all!

☆ Matthew 25:14-30

4.) God will honor faithfulness for an eternity

1.) Be faithful with what God gives you

Kingdom of Heaven - God's ruling over Earth

God has given us heavenly gifts & expects us to use them

When others experience your gift, they should experience the Kingdom of heaven

2.) Don't play it safe

Yellow = God (Van Gogh)

✗ See your environment as your mission field

3.) Be faithful even when you're fearful

Courageous - Be faithful even when in fear

God goes before you

SESSION 4 — SMALL GROUP INTRO

Time is often regarded as the most important resource on the planet. Once gone, it cannot be altered. There is no way to double it or increase it in the presence. And despite how hard we try, there is no guarantee of how much we possess in the future. So how can we surrender our past, present, and future to the Lord when it seems like we have no control over our time anyways?

This is a great question, and one that you could even spend your life trying to answer. What you will hopefully see in this short time together is that total surrender of our past, present, and future is mostly about how we use and view that time. When you surrender your life to Christ, you no longer have to look back on your past with shame. You no longer have to worry about what your future looks like. And in every moment, you are continually allowing God to show you how to live more like Him an less like the world.

GETTING STARTED
SESSION 4

Match the famous surrender with the year that it occurred!

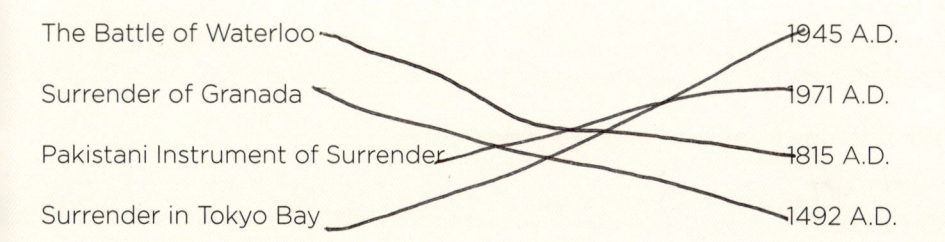

The Battle of Waterloo —————————————— 1945 A.D.

Surrender of Granada —————————————— 1971 A.D.

Pakistani Instrument of Surrender —————————————— 1815 A.D.

Surrender in Tokyo Bay —————————————— 1492 A.D.

INTERESTING FACTS:

The Pakistani Instrument of Surrender gave 93,000 Pakistani soldiers to India, which was the largest surrender of soldiers since WWII.

The Surrender of Granada ended the religious face-off between the Nasrid Kingdom of Granada and the monarchs of Argon and Castile. At the time, this changed the religious landscape of the Iberian Peninsula.

The Battle of Waterloo was the final blow to Napoleon's conquest for Europe. After suffering defeat, he fled back to Paris.

The Surrender in Tokyo Bay marked the end of WWII, as well as Japan's military campaigns throughout Asia. It is often regarded as one of the most extravagant surrender ceremonies. It took place on the U.S.S Missouri.

DIGGING IN
SESSION 4

Read Philippians 3:12-16 with your group.

Not that I have already obtained this or am already perfect, but I press on to make it my own, because Christ Jesus has made me his own. Brothers, I do not consider that I have made it my own. But one thing I do: forgetting what lies behind and straining forward to what lies ahead, I press on toward the goal for the prize of the upward call of God in Christ Jesus. Let those of us who are mature think this way, and if in anything you think otherwise, God will reveal that also to you. Only let us hold true to what we have attained.

- **What things from your past still haunt you?**

    Sexual sins

- **When you think of the word shame, what imagery do you associate with it?**

    Chains/Shackles holding me back & being scared

Read 1 John 1:9 with your group.

If we confess our sins, he is faithful and just to forgive us our sins and to cleanse us from all unrighteousness.

- **Think about the last time you confessed a sin to God. Was it difficult? How did you feel afterwards?**

    last night — Relieved

- **What do you believe it means when we talk about God being faithful to forgive us?**

    He never leaves us

Read John 15:8-11 with your group.

By this my Father is glorified, that you bear much fruit and so prove to be my disciples. As the Father has loved me, so have I loved you. Abide in my love. If you keep my commandments, you will abide in my love, just as I have kept my Father's commandments and abide in his love. These things I have spoken to you, that my joy may be in you, and that your joy may be full.

- Let's make a quick connection between the beginning of this passage and the end. One of the fruits of the Spirit is joy. And if you look at the last line, Jesus is talking about having full joy in the Lord. What other connections do you see in this passage?

    Fruit of spirit = joy

- Why do you think it is important to God that we abide in His love and bear fruit for others to see?

    To spread his joy & fruit

Read Matthew 11:28-30 with your group.

Come to me, all who labor and are heavy laden, and I will give you rest. Take my yoke upon you, and learn from me, for I am gentle and lowly in heart, and you will find rest for your souls. For my yoke is easy, and my burden is light.

- What do you believe Jesus is calling you to in this passage?

    To follow him & he will take care of you

- How does that differ from what the world calls you to?

    The world says to give into your pleasures/desires

WRAPPING UP — SESSION 4

Total Surrender to Christ looks like being_____ with Christ.

- What does that mean in your life? Have you been crucified with Christ?

Total Surrender means that it is now _____ who lives in me.

- What does it look like when Christ lives in someone? What are some ways that you see Christ living through you?

Total Surrender is believing that Christ _____ me, and_____ _____ for me.

- Take a moment to let those words sink in. Jesus loves you to the point that He gave Himself to the Cross for you. As you reflect on this, write some of your thoughts below.

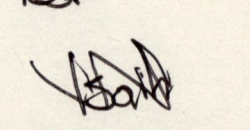

Isaiah 41:13

CLOSING

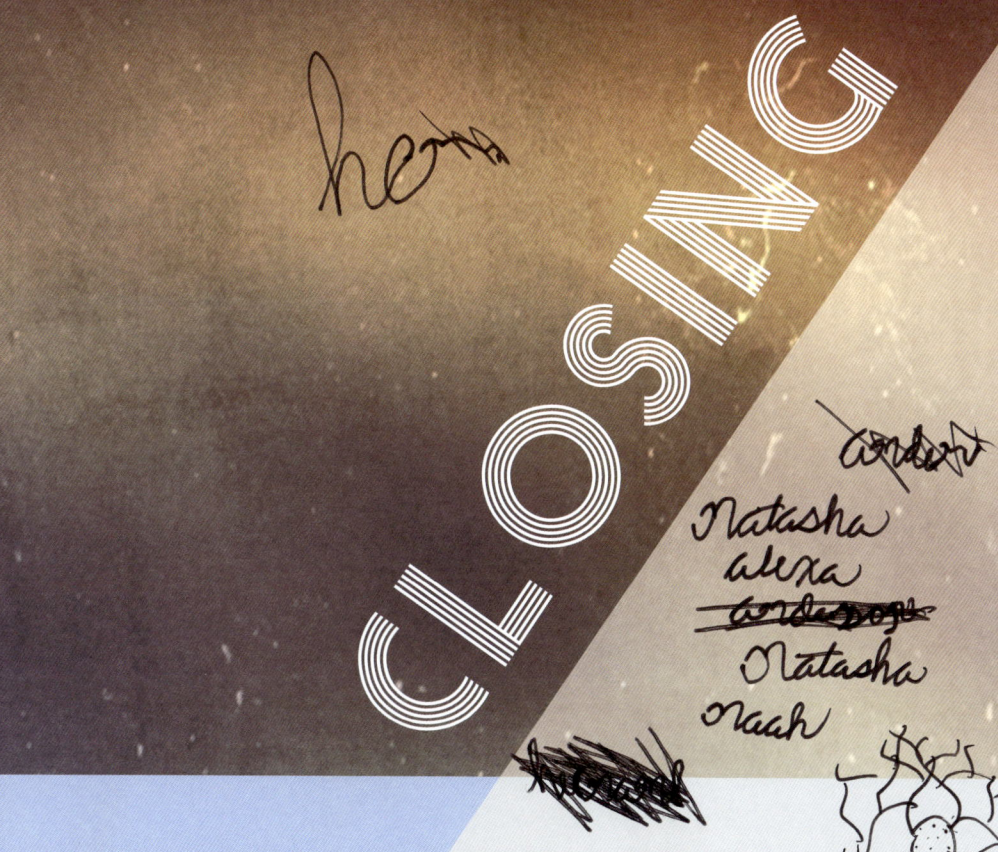

Giving everything to God is exactly what *Total Surrender* is all about.

Everything in our minds, hearts, and souls is meant to be His. And that may sound scary because, in our world, being an individual is greatly valued. Don't get it wrong- God has created you wonderfully unique and is not looking to conform you to a boring, sad version of yourself. Hopefully, what you have learned over the past four sessions is that God wants you to take everything that makes you special and surrender it to Him. He has much bigger plans for you than you could ever come up with or accomplish on your own.

When we hear the word surrender, we often think of a loss. We see surrender as a last resort. But that is what makes surrendering to God so special! The only thing you lose is the things that are holding you back. Things like shame, guilt, and confusion. And once those are gone and you've embraced a new life in Christ, you gain far more than can be counted. You gain spiritual fruits, a renewed relationship with the Creator of the world, and an eternal home that nobody can ever take from you (to name just a few).

So, ask yourself: have I taken part in *Total Surrender*?

DEVOTION 1

For my thoughts are not your thoughts, neither are your ways my ways," declares the LORD. "As the heavens are higher than the earth, so are my ways higher than your ways and my thoughts than your thoughts" (Isaiah 55:8-9)

If you one of the youngest in your group, then you are probably sick and tired of hearing that everyone else knows best. Maybe you tried to get a game going earlier, and just as you were feeling like you had it all under control, some kid in high school swooped in and tried to take over.

Or maybe you are the high schooler who wanted to show all of the newer people the best spot to sit during the service. And as you are instructing them to sit in that second-to-front row, one of your adult leaders redirects everyone to sit somewhere else. It's the classic case of someone saying "I know better" without really saying it. And it can be frustrating... especially if you had a great idea.

Our whole lives will be filled with people who claim to know better. Some of them really do know better, but some of them do not. Part of growing up is finding a way to figure out which is which, and then deciding how to respond accordingly. This is called discernment (which sounds like 'dis-urn-mint'). And do you know who has the best discernment of all? God!

READ ISAIAH 55:8-9.

In these two verses, God is flexing in a way that none of us ever could. He is basically saying "From my vantage point up here in the heavens, I can see far more than you can even imagine." You can spend your whole life gaining knowledge, but you will not be able to look out across time and space the way that God can.

Total Surrender to God begins with understanding that He truly knows more than we are able. And He is not using that to harm us or make us look dumb. Instead, He is inviting us to trust His knowledge and follow Him even when it doesn't make sense to us at the time. Because He really does know better!

FOLLOW-UP QUESTIONS

1. Think about the last time that you tried to teach someone something new. What was that experience like, and did they learn what you wanted them to?

2. What has God called you to surrender to Him so far?

3. Based on Isaiah 55:8-9, we understand that God knows far more than we ever could. If you could ask God one BIG question, what would it be?

DEVOTION 2

Grace to you and peace from God our Father and the Lord Jesus Christ, who gave himself for our sins to deliver us from the present evil age, according to the will of our God and Father. (Galatians 1:3-4)

The Bible tells us that God made mankind in His own image (Genesis 1:27 and John 1:1-5). And when God created humanity, He created us to act righteously, just like Him. That means that what we do would be 'right' in His eyes. In fact, the first job that humans had in the Garden of Eden was to rule over all of what God created (Genesis 1:28-31). That is a lot of responsibility, and God trusted us with it because He created us to be kind, gentle, faithful, and patient (these are righteous behaviors).

But one day, Adam and Eve decided that they wanted something else. They felt that God was withholding something from them- specifically the knowledge of unrighteousness, or as we may better know it: evil. Not caring about the consequence it would have for their children, Adam and Eve rebelled against God's rules for righteous living. They pursued God's knowledge of good and evil, even though He warned that it would lead to death. And ever since that original sin, humanity has been cursed. Instead of being righteous as God intended, we are born with sin on our minds and in our hearts. And nothing in our own power can break this curse. We are now fully tainted with the knowledge and desire for unrighteous things.

READ GALATIANS 1:3-4.

Thankfully, Jesus has made it possible to be reborn. You do not have to remain stuck in the sin (unrighteousness) that you were born into. You may be wondering how somebody could be reborn, which is a question that was even asked by someone in the Bible (check out John 3:4-7). But before you can put away your old life and start living in the new one, you must totally surrender to Jesus. This involves confessing that Jesus Christ did exactly what He says He did- take on the curse of sin that we deserve (which is death) so that we can live a new life in Him.

Surrendering to Jesus means that you are telling yourself and others "I am not able to be who God intended for me to be on my own. I need Him to make that happen." And that is a powerful statement. It is not only admitting that you understand the role sin plays in your life, but it is proclaiming that without Christ, you would not have any hope of a life apart from sin.

FOLLOW-UP QUESTIONS

1. What are some ways that sin has impacted your life so far?

    Sin has made me deceitful & corrupted my heart

2. God understands that we could not be righteous on our own. If He left us alone in this state, He could remain unbothered in Heaven while we suffered from the results of our own sins. Why do you think Jesus chose to do something as painful as death on a Cross so that you could have a chance to be righteous again?

    Because he loves us

3. Do you think that you would have done that if you were in God's position?

    No

DEVOTION 3

If then you have been raised with Christ, seek the things that are above, where Christ is, seated at the right hand of God. (Colossians 3:1)

Going to the dentist stinks. Sure, you usually come out of the dentist with healthier gums and teeth. But there are very few people in the world that enjoy having their mouth held open so that a little metal stick can root around and remove the gunk between their teeth. And so, what do you do when you are sitting in the chair and the person cleaning your teeth is carrying on about good flossing habits? You try to distract yourself by thinking of other things.

The human mind is really incredible. It can travel to far off places without taking a single step. It can learn to multi-task or focus intensely on one thing. There are so many things that our minds can think about, because that is how God created us. And knowing that our minds can do both incredible and also very dangerous things, God has asked something of us that will help us leave behind our old lives and embrace the new life that can only be found in Him.

READ COLOSSIANS 3:1.

God is asking for us to seek out the things above, or the things of Heaven. Think back to the dentist office. You may just as easily think about the snack you're going to have when you get home, or you could have imagined a place that you've never been to. The point was that even though you were present in one place, in your mind, you were already somewhere else.

When we practice totally surrendering to God, we understand that this world is more like the dentist office. Sure, it's not always the most uncomfortable place we could be. But ultimately, we would love to be somewhere else. Our minds are with God, and we are thinking about eternal life with Him. This is one of the most important steps in surrendering our day to day moments to the Lord. Everything that you do will point back to whether or not you have your mind set on the ways of God. And the more that you display the works of God here on Earth, the less and less it feels like there is such a big distance between the two!

FOLLOW-UP QUESTIONS

1. Think about everything you've done since waking up this morning. How many of those things do you think show others that you are seeking things above?

   By remaining positive though it's early

2. Sometimes Jesus calls us to do things that the world doesn't understand. What is something that God has called you to do, even though you know others may judge you?

   Jesus has called me to take care of children h & "settle down" Carly

3. What are some examples of 'things above' and how they are different than the things you see in the world around you?

   Being humble, always looking forward h being wise. This is different because people boast h are full of envy.

DEVOTION 4

The end of the matter; all has been heard. Fear God and keep his commandments, for this is the whole duty of man. (Ecclesiastes 12:13)

As we close out this time together, let's talk about what happens next. If you have totally surrendered your life to God, that has huge implications for both your past, present, and future. Earlier, you likely talked about surrendering your past to God in the form of receiving forgiveness for all of your past sin. This is only possible through the work of Jesus Christ on the Cross. In the present, followers of Christ surrender their old (or sinful) ways of thinking and living and instead live as God instructs us. This is done by reading Scripture and by growing in the Holy Spirit.

You will probably encounter a moment very soon where you want to surrender to God, but you aren't sure how. It could be deciding what career path to follow, who to date, or even where to live. When there seems to be no right or wrong answer, it can be difficult to determine what God is calling you to do.

READ ECCLESIASTES 12:13.

What this verse wants you to understand is that God want following Him to be way simpler than we sometimes try to make it. If you are ever overwhelmed, come back to this verse and remember that your primary duty as a follower of Christ is to fear God and keep His commandments.

There are so many things that God may call you to do over the course of your life. But you will never be left with nothing to do. If you have a friend who has a calling to go on mission in a different country, or a sibling that is called to be a pastor, it can be tempting to look at your own life and think "why won't God call me to something meaningful already?" And the answer to that question is that He already has! When Jesus called His disciples, He did not tell them exactly what they would be doing for the next few years. In fact, He barely told them anything at all! His only request was that they leave behind their old lives and follow Him.

God is calling you to the same kind of life. Yes, He may call you to a specific form of ministry. And if He does, that is AWESOME. But He may also call you to walk with Him a while, and never fully tell you where you are going. And that is awesome too! Whatever God has in store for you, remember this verse in Ecclesiastes. Every day that you wake up, regardless of where you are and when, your duty is to fear God and follow His commandments. Are you up to it?

FOLLOW-UP QUESTIONS

1. What are some of the things that you can do to live like Ecclesiastes 12:13?

2. How does fearing God and following His commandments relate to total surrender?

3. Take a moment to think of one big message that God has spoken to you this week. Try to sum it up in one sentence, and write it below.

HOW TO KNOW JESUS

Maybe you've turned to this page having never entered into a saving relationship with Jesus. Maybe you already have a saving relationship with Jesus and need to be more committed to making Him known. No matter where you find yourself, this page is for you. If you need to know Jesus, this page is an excellent place to start. If you need to make Jesus known, this page can help you think about how to go about sharing His story with others.

TO ENTER INTO A SAVING RELATIONSHIP WITH JESUS, YOU FIRST HAVE TO UNDERSTAND WHO GOD IS.

First, God is the Creator (Gen 1:1). He created everything, even you. Second, God is perfect in all His ways (Ps. 18:30). So, combined, that makes God the perfect creator of all things. He rules over everything, and His rule is 100% right.

NEXT, YOU HAVE TO ACCEPT THAT YOUR SIN IS A PROBLEM (ONE THAT YOU CANT SOLVE ON YOUR OWN).

Because God is the perfect King, when we do something that goes against His ways, it's called sin. And because God is who He is, all sin is rebellion against Him (Ps. 51:3-4). The only right penalty for our rebellion? It's death (Rom. 6:23). Both spiritual and physical. The worst part is that we're completely unable to save ourselves.

THEN, YOU HAVE TO GRASP THE TRUTH THAT JESUS IS THE ONLY ANSWER TO YOUR SIN PROBLEM.

Jesus was God's Son, sent to earth to live a perfect life that He might serve as the once-and-for-all perfect sacrifice in our place (Matt. 1:18-21). Jesus died on the cross to satisfy God's sense of justice and save from their sins all who will believe in Him (John 3:16). Only Jesus could do this.

FINALLY, YOU HAVE TO BELIEVE IN YOUR HEART THAT JESUS IS WHO HE SAYS HE IS AND THAT HIS DEATH ACCOMPLISHED WHAT HE SAID IT ACCOMPLISHED.

The only way that we can be saved from our sin problem is to believe that Jesus is who He says He is. When we put our faith in Jesus as our Savior, we're saved from the penalty of our sin. We're saved from death. This is only possible by God's grace through faith in Jesus. We can't do anything to earn our salvation. Here's the coolest part: When you come to salvation in Christ, your life is completely renewed, freed from the effects of sin (2 Cor. 5:17). You are a new creation!

IF YOU NEED TO COME TO FAITH IN JESUS, LET THESE WORDS GUIDE YOU. AND IF YOU KNOW SOMEONE THAT NEEDS CHRIST, USE THIS TO HELP YOU SHARE THE GOSPEL WITH THEM.

ACKNOWLEDGEMENTS

EDITORIAL:
AMBER WARREN: WRITER & MANAGING EDITOR

KERRY RAY: DIRECTOR OF PUBLISHING

DESIGN:
MORGAN WILLIAMS

FTN DESIGN

A 3-PART DEVOTIONAL EXPERIENCE
DESIGNED TO HELP YOU BECOME A DISCIPLE OF CHRIST.

NEW: FIRST STEPS FOR NEW CHRIST-FOLLOWERS

A powerful 4-week experience to help you get off to a strong start on our journey with Jesus. Build a firm foundation by understanding what changes when you are alive with Jesus.

NEXT: GROWING A FAITH THAT LASTS

4-weeks to guide you in taking ownership of your faith. What is life's purpose and what it has to do with God's mission. Learn to implement spiritual habits to transform you life.

NOW: IMPACTING YOUR WORLD FOR CHRIST (RIGHT NOW!)

Do not wait until later to make an impact for Jesus, you can do it NOW! This 4-week experience will open your eyes to the everyday opportunities you have to live for Jesus NOW!, not just in the future.

YM360.COM/DISCIPLESHIP-BUNDLE
to order or download a free sample